SpringerBriefs in Computer Science

Series Editors
Stan Zdonik
Peng Ning
Shashi Shekhar
Jonathan Katz
Xindong Wu
Lakhmi C. Jain
David Padua
Xuemin Shen
Borko Furht

For further volumes:
http://www.springer.com/series/10028

Dhruv Batra • Adarsh Kowdle • Devi Parikh
Jiebo Luo • Tsuhan Chen

Interactive Co-segmentation of Objects in Image Collections

Dhruv Batra
Toyota Technological Institute
Chicago
Illinois, USA

Devi Parikh
Toyota Technological Institute
Chicago
Illinois, USA

Tsuhan Chen
Cornell University
Ithaca
New York, USA

Adarsh Kowdle
Cornell University
Ithaca
New York, USA

Jiebo Luo
University of Rochester
Rochester
New York, USA

ISSN 2191-5768   e-ISSN 2191-5776
ISBN 978-1-4614-1914-3   e-ISBN 978-1-4614-1915-0
DOI 10.1007/978-1-4614-1915-0
Springer New York Dordrecht Heidelberg London

Library of Congress Control Number: 2011941116

Printed on acid-free paper

Springer is part of Springer Science+Business Media (www.springer.com)

Preface

We survey a recent technique in computer vision called Co-segmentation, which is the task of simultaneously extracting (or co-segmenting) common foreground objects from multiple related images. The notion of co-segmentation was originally introduced several years ago, and has since been extended in various ways.

In this manuscript, we review a number of these recent techniques in Chapter 1. We present one technique for interactive co-segmentation, our recent work called iCoseg in detail in Chapter 2. We provide an overview of applications of object co-segmentation in Chapter 3 and finally discuss some exciting future directions in Chapter 4.

We hope this manuscript gives the reader a combination of breadth and depth on this topic, and will serve as a good introductory reference for the problem of co-segmentation.

Chicago IL, Aug 2011 *-Authors*

Acknowledgements

The authors would like to thank Yu-Wei Chao for data collection and annotation. This dataset has been extensively used in several experiments discussed in this book, and since its first introduction has been widely used in co-segmentation literature. We would also like to thank Kevin Tang for developing the java-based GUI (iScrrible) used in the user-studies described in this book. It also forms the basis of many demonstrations of our interactive co-segmentation system.

We are also grateful for the assistance provided by Jennifer Maurer and the publication team at SpringerBriefs.

Contents

Chapter 1
Introduction

Abstract In this chapter, we introduce the problem of co-segmentation and survey some recent algorithms for co-segmentation. We organize these algorithms along two dimensions – degree of supervision and scalability. Finally, we comment on connections between interactive co-segmentation and (single image) interactive segmentation and video cutout.

1.1 Overview of Co-segmentation

We live in a highly photographed world. By most estimates, there are more than a Billion camera-phones in use in the world. As of August 2011, photosharing websites like Flickr and Facebook boast of hosting 5 and 50 Billion photos respectively, with millions more added every month. Consumers typically have several related pictures of the same object, event or destination, and this rich collection is just waiting to be exploited by vision researchers – from something as simple as building a collage of all the foregrounds, to something more sophisticated like a constructing the complete 3D model of a particular object. In many such tasks, it would be useful to extract a common foreground object from all images in a group of related images. This *co-segmentation* of foreground objects from multiple related images is the focus of this book.

Formally, the setup is as follows: we are given a set of images $\mathcal{I} = \{I^{(1)}, \ldots, I^{(n)}\}$ all containing a common foreground object and the goal is to simultaneously produce segmentations, *i.e.* foreground background labellings $\mathcal{X} = \{X^{(1)}, \ldots, X^{(n)}\}$ for this set.

The problem of co-segmentation was introduced by Rother *et al.* [17] in a fairly restricted setting. Since then, however, various authors [3–5, 7, 10–12, 14, 15, 18, 19] have expanded on their initial framework in various ways. In the next section, we review a number of these recent techniques and organize them along two axes: degree of supervision and scalability.

1.2 Organizing Co-segmentation Algorithms

Perhaps the best way to map the landscape of co-segmentation algorithms is to categorize them by the degree of supervision involved:

1. Unsupervised co-segmentation, which takes as input only a group of related images,
2. Interactive co-segmentation, which takes as input a group of related images *and* a sparse set of pixels labelled via scribbles, user strokes, or bounding box annotations and
3. Supervised co-segmentation, which takes as input a group of related images and a complete (pixel-level) segmentation on a few images.

Another pragmatic dimension to characterize co-segmentation algorithms is the issue of scalability, *i.e.* whether the algorithms displays a linear or super-linear growth in run-time as a function of the number of images in the group. We organize co-segmentation algorithms along both these dimensions next.

1.2.1 Unsupervised vs. Interactive vs. Supervised Co-segmentation

Unsupervised Co-segmentation. Most existing works on co-segmentation [7, 10–12, 14, 15, 17–19] can be described as unsupervised co-segmentation techniques. Thus, these techniques assume access to only a group of related images and no supervision. The common central idea in a number of these approaches [10, 14, 15, 17, 18] is to formulate co-segmentation as an energy minimization based binary labelling problem . A single energy function is defined over all pixels in all images in a group. This energy function consists of the usual Markov Random Field (MRF) smoothness prior that encourage smooth segmentations in each image, and importantly, a histogram matching term, that penalizes dissimilarity between foreground histograms of images in the group. Thus, by minimizing this energy function, these methods jointly segment (or co-segment) all images in the group such these co-segmentations are both smooth and have similar appearance in the foreground regions.

Rother *et al.* [17] introduced the problem of (unsupervised) co-segmentation of image pairs via an energy function with a particular histogram matching term. Mukherjee *et al.* [14] proposed half-integrality algorithms for minimizing the energy function. Singh and Hochbaum [10] modified the histogram matching term to propose max-flow based algorithms. Vicente *et al.* [18] conducted a comparative evaluation of various histogram matching terms. Mukherjee *et al.* [15] proposed a histogram matching term that is able to perform scale-invariant co-segmentation, *i.e.* invariant to the size of the foreground objects in different images.

Different from the energy minimization techniques, Joulin *et al.* [11] formulated unsupervised co-segmentation in a discriminative clustering framework where the

(a) Stone-pair [17].   (b) Taj-Mahal-pair from the CMU-Cornell iCoseg Dataset [3].

Fig. 1.1: What is foreground? The stone-pair (a) has significant variation in background with nearly identical foreground and thus unsupervised co-segmentation can easily extract the stone as foreground. The Taj-Mahal-pair is fairly consistent as a whole and thus the Taj Mahal cannot be cut out via unsupervised co-segmentation. Bringing a user in the loop is necessary for the problem of foreground extraction to be well defined.

goal is to label all image regions as foreground or background, such that a classifier trained with these labels produces maximum separation between the classes. Vicente *et al.* [19] propose the first "object" co-segmentation algorithm that, despite being an unsupervised algorithm (and thus being unaware of the entity being co-segmented), attempts to produce object-like foreground segments. Kim *et al.* [12] propose the first multiclass (K-way) unsupervised co-segmentation algorithm based on temperature maximization on anisotropic heat diffusion. The proposed algorithm is also the first distributed algorithm for co-segmentation. Chai *et al.* [7] propose a two-level unsupervised co-segmentation algorithm that iterates between segmenting images independently and using the produced segmentations to learn an SVM classifier separating foreground from background.

The common theme in unsupervised co-segmentation is enforcing consistency in appearance of segmented foregrounds. This approach however requires the dataset to be chosen with care because it would fail for pairs/groups with similar backgrounds (see Fig. 1.1), where the problem of identifying the "foreground" objects is ill-posed. In practice, these methods typically work with a pair (or group) of images with similar (sometimes nearly identical) foreground, and unrelated backgrounds. For example, the "Stone-pair" in Fig. 1.1 has significant variation in background with nearly identical foreground and thus unsupervised co-segmentation methods can easily extract the stone as foreground. This property is necessary because the goal of these works is to extract the common foreground object *automatically*, without any user-input. The Taj-Mahal-pair, on the other hand, is fairly consistent as a whole and thus the Taj Mahal cannot be cut out via unsupervised co-segmentation methods. Bringing a user in the loop is necessary for the problem of foreground extraction to be well defined in this case. As we argue in Chapter 2, the latter case is more common in typical consumer photo collections.

This is where *interactive* co-segmentation techniques fit in, which allow a user to indicate the foreground objects through simple scribbles.

Interactive Co-segmentation. Interactive co-segmentation methods bring a user "into the loop" by allowing the user to label a sparse set of pixels via some user interface. To the best of our knowledge, so far, there exists only one interactive co-segmentation system in the literature – iCoseg [3, 4]. We describe this technique in detail in Chapter 2.

Supervised Co-segmentation. At the end of the supervision spectrum are *supervised* co-segmentation algorithms, that require as input not just a few scribbled pixels, but complete segmentations for a few (training) images, which are then used to learn appearance models for the classes.

Cui *et al.* [9] proposed a transductive algorithm that uses the complete segmentations to learn a local colour pattern descriptor for foreground and an edge-profile model for foreground-background edges. Note that neither of these powerful descriptors would be possible to learn from scribbles, let alone completely unsupervised, because they require complete knowledge of foreground and background.

1.2.2 Linear vs Super-linear Runtime

We now try to organize co-segmentation algorithms according to their scalability, specifically, the growth in their runtime as a function of the number of images (n) in the group. We argue that it is important to distinguish algorithms that guarantee linear (or sub-linear) growth from the ones that exhibit super-linear (*e.g.* quadratic) growth. As n becomes large, which in modern image collections it typically does, super-linear run-times can quickly become hopelessly impractical.

Super-Linear Co-segmentation Algorithms. All co-segmentation techniques that optimize a single global objective function for the entire group of images [10, 14, 15, 17, 18] (with the exception of Mukherjee *et al.* [15]) are super-linear in n. They construct a graph where each pixel (or superpixel) in each image is connected to *all* pixels (or superpixels) in all other images. Thus, just constructing this graph takes quadratic time in n.

Joulin *et al.* [11] formulate their unsupervised co-segmentation algorithm as a semi-definite program (SDP), but propose various optimization tricks to reduce the complexity of solving this SDP to $O(n^2)$. The algorithms of Vicente *et al.* [19] and Kim *et al.* [12], although fairly dissimilar, both require solving an inference problem on a fully connected MRF where each image is a node in the graph. While this approach is considerably more efficient than methods that construct a graph where each *pixel* (or superpixel) is a node, it is still super-linear in n.

Linear Co-segmentation Algorithms. The algorithms of Cui *et al.* [9] and Batra *et al.* [3, 4] are both linear time co-segmentation algorithms. Both the approaches employ a similar high-level strategy – they learn an appearance model for foreground and background from the labelled pixels, and then decouple the segmentation process in different images via this shared appearance model. The algorithms of Mukherjee *et al.* [15] and Chai *et al.* [7], although vastly different in details, may be seen as a generalization of this idea – their iterative algorithms alternate between fitting an appearance models and producing decoupled segmentations in each image. Thus, if the number of iterations is assumed constant (or independent of n), their algorithms are also linear in n.

1.3 Historical Perspective: Interactive Co-segmentation as a Generalization of Interactive Image and Video Cutout

The problem of co-segmentation, specifically interactive co-segmentation, can be understood as a generalization of two other problems in computer vision – image cutout and video cutout.

Interactive single-image segmentation (or image cutout) has a long history in computer vision. Boykov and Jolly [6] provided a very general energy minimization framework for the problem that is at the heart of most recent techniques. A user typically provides foreground/background scribbles [6, 13] or a coarse bounding-box [16] of the object of interest in the image. The algorithm uses this information to not only learn foreground/background appearance models for this image, but also as hard constraints for some pixels, which typically makes the energy minimization problem easier. There have been many improvements since, *e.g.* Bai and Sapiro [1] and Criminisi *et al.* [8] proposed techniques built on efficient geodesic distance computations, and this list is by no means exhaustive.

Interactive co-segmentation is thus a natural generalization to multiple images. However, there are issues that warrant some care. In a single-image setup, a user visually inspects the produced cutout and gives more scribbles to correct mistakes made by the algorithm. However, this approach would not work for interactive co-segmentation because 1) as the number of images in the group increases, it becomes increasingly cumbersome for a user to iterate through all the images in the group to find the worst segmentation; and 2) even if the user were willing to identify an incorrect cutout, there might be multiple incorrect cutouts in the group, some more confusing to the segmentation algorithm than others. Observing labels on the most confusing ones first would help reduce the number of user annotations required. It is thus necessary for the algorithm to be able to suggest regions in images where scribbles would be the most informative.

The problem of interactive video cutout, *i.e.* extracting a foreground object from a video sequence instead of an image has also seen a number of advances [1,2,6,20]. Interactive co-segmentation can be seen as a generalization of video cutout because it involves object cutout from a volume, albeit with the loss of temporal continuity.

Having provided a broad overview of the problem and various techniques addressing co-segmentation, in the following chapter we now provide an in-depth description of one particular approach to interactive co-segmentation: iCoseg [3].

References

1. X. Bai and G. Sapiro. A geodesic framework for fast interactive image and video segmentation and matting. In *ICCV*, 2007.
2. X. Bai, J. Wang, D. Simons, and G. Sapiro. Video snapcut: robust video object cutout using localized classifiers. In *ACM SIGGRAPH*, pages 70:1–70:11, 2009.
3. D. Batra, A. Kowdle, D. Parikh, J. Luo, and T. Chen. icoseg: Interactive co-segmentation with intelligent scribble guidance. In *CVPR*, 2010.
4. D. Batra, A. Kowdle, D. Parikh, J. Luo, and T. Chen. Interactively co-segmentating topically related images with intelligent scribble guidance. *International Journal of Computer Vision*, To Appear, 2011.
5. D. Batra, D. Parikh, A. Kowdle, T. Chen, and J. Luo. Seed image selection in interactive cosegmentation. In *ICIP*, 2009.
6. Y. Boykov and M.-P. Jolly. Interactive graph cuts for optimal boundary and region segmentation of objects in n-d images. *ICCV*, 2001.
7. Y. Chai, V. Lempitsky, and A. Zisserman. Bicos: A bi-level co-segmentation method for image classification. In *ICCV*, 2011.
8. A. Criminisi, T. Sharp, and A. Blake. Geos: Geodesic image segmentation. In *ECCV*, 2008.
9. J. Cui, Q. Yang, F. Wen, Q. Wu, C. Zhang, L. V. Gool, and X. Tang. Transductive object cutout. In *CVPR*, 2008.
10. D. S. Hochbaum and V. Singh. An efficient algorithm for co-segmentation. In *ICCV*, 2009.
11. A. Joulin, F. R. Bach, and J. Ponce. Discriminative clustering for image co-segmentation. In *CVPR*, pages 1943–1950, 2010.
12. G. Kim, E. P. Xing, L. Fei-Fei, and T. Kanade. Distributed cosegmentation via submodular optimization on anisotropic diffusion. In *ICCV*, 2011.
13. Y. Li, J. Sun, C.-K. Tang, and H.-Y. Shum. Lazy snapping. *SIGGRAPH*, 2004.
14. L. Mukherjee, V. Singh, and C. R. Dyer. Half-integrality based algorithms for cosegmentation of images. In *CVPR*, 2009.
15. L. Mukherjee, V. Singh, and J. Peng. Scale invariant cosegmentation for image groups. In *CVPR*, 2011.
16. C. Rother, V. Kolmogorov, and A. Blake. "Grabcut": interactive foreground extraction using iterated graph cuts. *SIGGRAPH*, 2004.
17. C. Rother, T. Minka, A. Blake, and V. Kolmogorov. Cosegmentation of image pairs by histogram matching - incorporating a global constraint into mrfs. In *CVPR*, 2006.
18. S. Vicente, V. Kolmogorov, and C. Rother. Cosegmentation revisited: Models and optimization. In *ECCV*, 2010.
19. S. Vicente, C. Rother, and V. Kolmogorov. Object cosegmentation. In *CVPR*, 2011.
20. J. Wang, P. Bhat, R. A. Colburn, M. Agrawala, and M. F. Cohen. Interactive video cutout. *ACM Trans. Graph.*, 24:585–594, July 2005.

Chapter 2
An Approach to Interactive Co-segmentation

Abstract In this chapter, we describe in detail our approach to interactive co-segmentation. We formulate the task as an energy minimization problem across all related images in a group. The energies across images are tied together via a shared appearance model, thus allowing for efficient inference. After describing our formulation, we present an active learning approach that makes efficient use of users' time. A wide variety of cues are combined to intelligently guide the users' next scribbles. We then introduce our co-segmentation dataset, The CMU-Cornell iCoseg dataset, the largest of its kind to date. We evaluate our system on this dataset using machine simulations as well as real user-studies. We find that our approach can achieve comparable co-segmentation performance with less user effort.

2.1 Energy Minimization

Our approach [3] to multiple-image interactive co-segmentation is a natural extension of [7]. Given user scribbles indicating foreground / background, we cast our labelling problem as minimization of Gibbs energies defined over graphs constructed over each image in a group. Specifically, consider a group of m image-scribble pairs $D = \{(\mathscr{X}^{(1)}, \mathscr{S}^{(1)}), \ldots, (\mathscr{X}^{(m)}, \mathscr{S}^{(m)})\}$, where the kth image is represented as a collection of n_k sites to be labelled, $i.e.$ $\mathscr{X}^{(k)} = \{X_1^{(k)}, X_2^{(k)}, \ldots, X_{n_k}^{(k)}\}$, and scribbles for an image $\mathscr{S}^{(k)}$ are represented as the partial (potentially empty)[1] set of labels for these sites. For computational efficiency, we use superpixels as these labelling sites (instead of pixels).[2] For each image (k), we build a graph, $\mathscr{G}^{(k)} = (\mathscr{V}^{(k)}, \mathscr{E}^{(k)})$, over superpixels, with edges connecting adjacent superpixels.

---

[1] Specifically, we require at least one labelled foreground and background site to train our models, but only one per *group*, not per image.

[2] We use mean-shift [10] to extract these superpixels, and typically break down 350×500 images into 400 superpixels per image.

At the start of our algorithm, we require at least one foreground and background scribble each. They can be in the same image, or in multiple images. Subsequent iterations can have a scribble just from foreground or background. Using these labelled sites, we learn a group appearance model $\mathscr{A} = \{A_1, A_2\}$, where A_1 is the first-order (unary) appearance model, and A_2 the second-order (pairwise) appearance model. This appearance model ($\mathscr{A}$) is described in detail in the following sections. We note that all images in the group share a common model, *i.e.* only one model is learnt. Using this appearance model, we define a collection of energies over each of the m images as follows:

$$
E^{(k)}(\mathscr{X}^{(k)} : \mathscr{A}) = \sum_{i \in \mathscr{V}^{(k)}} E_i(X_i^{(k)} : A_1)
$$
$$
+ \lambda \sum_{(i,j) \in \mathscr{E}^{(k)}} E_{ij}\left(X_i^{(k)}, X_j^{(k)} : A_2\right), \tag{2.1}
$$

where the first term is the data term indicating the cost of assigning a superpixel to foreground and background classes, while the second term is the smoothness term used for penalizing label disagreement between neighbours. Note that the (:) part in these terms indicates that both these terms are functions of the learnt appearance model. From now on, to simplify notation, we write these terms as $E_i(X_i)$ and $E_{ij}(X_i, X_j)$, and the dependence on the appearance model $\mathscr{A}$ and image (k) is implicit.

2.1.1 Data (Unary) Term

Our unary appearance model consists of a foreground and background Gaussian Mixture Model, *i.e.*, $A_1 = \{GMM_f, GMM_b\}$. Specifically, we extract colour features extracted from superpixels (as proposed by [14]). We use features from labelled sites in all images to fit foreground and background GMMs (where number of gaussians was automatically learnt by minimizing an MDL criteria [6]). We then use these learnt GMMs to compute the data terms for all sites, which is the negative log-likelihood of the features given the class model.

2.1.2 Smoothness (Pairwise) Term

The most commonly used smoothness term in energy minimization based segmentation methods [11, 12, 21] is the contrast sensitive Potts model:

$$
E(X_i, X_j) = \mathrm{I}\,(X_i \neq X_j)\,\exp(-\beta d_{ij}), \tag{2.2}
$$

where I $(\cdot)$ is an indicator function that is 1(0) if the input argument is true(false), d_{ij} is the distance between features at superpixels i and j and β is a scale parameter. Intuitively, this smoothness term tries to penalize label discontinuities among neighbouring sites but modulates the penalty via a contrast-sensitive term. Thus, if two adjacent superpixels are far apart in the feature space, there would be a smaller cost for assigning them different labels than if they were close. However, as various authors have noted, this contrast sensitive modulation forces the segmentation to follow strong edges in the image, which might not necessarily correspond to object boundaries. For example, [12] modulate the distance d_{ij} based on statistics of edge profile features learnt from a fully segmented training image.

In this work, we use a distance metric learning algorithm to *learn* these d_{ij} from user scribbles. The basic intuition is that when two features (which might be far apart in Euclidean distance) are both labelled as the same class by the user scribbles, we want the distance between them to be low. Similarly, when two features are labelled as different classes, we want the distance between them to be large, even if they happen to be close by in Euclidean space. Thus, this new distance metric captures the pairwise statistics of the data better than Euclidean distance. For example, if colours blue and white were both scribbled as foreground, then the new distance metric would learn a small distance between them, and thus, a blue-white edge in the image would be heavily penalized for label discontinuity, while the standard contrast sensitive model would not penalize this edge as much. The specific choice of this algorithms is not important, and any state-of-art technique may be used. We use the implementation of [5].

We update both $A_1 = \{\text{GMM}_f, \text{GMM}_b\}$ and $A_2 = \{d_{ij}\}$ every time the user provides a new scribble. Finally, we note that contrast-sensitive potts model leads to a submodular energy function. We use graph-cuts to efficiently compute the MAP labels for all images, using the publicly available implementations of [1] and [8,9,16].

2.1.3 Comparing Energy Functions

Our introduced energy functions (2.1) are different from those typically found in co-segmentation literature and we make the following observations. While previous works [13,18,19,22] have formulated co-segmentation of image pairs with a single energy function, we assign to each image its own energy function. The reason we are able to do this is because we model the dependance between images implicitly via the common appearance model ($\mathscr{A}$), while previous works added an explicit histogram matching term to the common energy function. There are two distinct advantages of our approach. First, as several authors [13,18,19,22] have pointed out, adding an explicit histogram matching term makes the energy function intractable. On the other hand, each one of our energy functions is submodular and can be solved with a single graph-cut. Second, this common energy function grows at least quadratically with the number of images in the group, making these approaches almost impossible to scale to dozens of images in a group. On the other hand, given the appearance models, our collection of energy functions are completely independent. Thus the size of our problem only grows linearly in the number of images in the group, which is critical for interactive applications. In fact, each one of our energy functions may be optimized in parallel, making our approach amenable to distributed systems and multi-core architectures. Videos embedded on our project website [2] show our (single-core) implementation co-segmenting ~ 20 image in a matter of seconds.

To be fair, we should note that what allows us to set-up an efficiently solvable energy function is our incorporation of a user in the co-segmentation process, giving us partially labelled data (scribbles). While this user involvement is necessary because we work with globally related images, this involvement also means that the co-segmentation algorithm must be able to query/guide user scribbles, because users cannot be expected to examine all cutouts at each iteration. This is described next.

2.2 iCoseg: Guiding User Scribbles

In this section, we develop an intelligent recommendation algorithm to automatically seek user-scribbles and reduce the user effort. Given a set of initial scribbles from the user, we compute a recommendation map for each image in the group. The image (and region) with the highest recommendation score is presented to the user to receive more scribbles. Instead of committing to a single confusion measure as our recommendation score, which might be noisy, we use a number of "cues". These cues are then combined to form a final recommendation map, as seen in Fig. 2.1. The three categories of cues we use, and our approach to learning the weights of the combination are described next.

2.2.1 Uncertainty-based Cues

Node Uncertianty (NU): Our first cue is the one most commonly used in uncertainty sampling, *i.e.*, entropy of the node beliefs. Recall that each time scribbles are received, we fit $A_1 = \{\text{GMM}_f, \text{GMM}_b\}$ to the labelled superpixel features. Using this learnt A_1, for each superpixel we normalize the foreground and background likelihoods to get a 2-class distribution and then compute the entropy of this distribution. The intuition behind this cue is that the more uniform the class distribution for a site, the more we would like to observe its label.

Edge Uncertainty (EU): The Query by Committee [23] algorithm is a fundamental work that forms the basis for many selective sampling works. The simple but elegant idea is to feed unlabelled data-points to a committee/set of classifiers and request

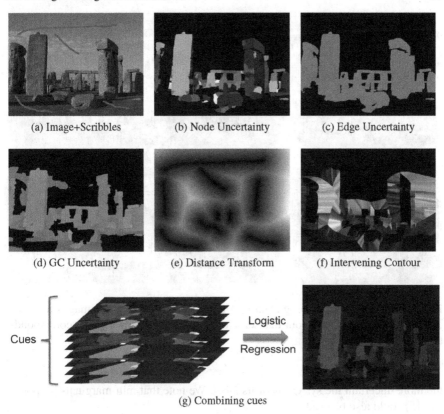

(a) Image+Scribbles　　　　(b) Node Uncertainty　　　　(c) Edge Uncertainty

(d) GC Uncertainty　　　　(e) Distance Transform　　　　(f) Intervening Contour

(g) Combining cues

Fig. 2.1: Cues: (a) shows the image with provided scribbles; (b)-(f) show various cues; and (g) shows how these cues are combined to produce a final recommendation map.

label for the data-point with maximal disagreement among classifier outcomes. We use this intuition to define our next cue. For each superpixel, we use our learnt distances (recall: these are used to define the edge smoothness terms in our energy function) to find K (=10) nearest neighbours from the labelled superpixels. We treat the proportion of each class in the returned list as the probability of assigning that class to this site, and use the entropy of this distribution as our cue. The intuition behind this cue is that the more uniform this distribution, the more disagreement there is among the the returned neighbour labels, and the more we would like to observe the label of this site.

Graph-cut Uncertainty (GC): This cue tries to capture the confidence in the energy minimizing state returned by graph-cuts. For each site, we compute the increase in energy by flipping the optimal assignment at that site. The intuition behind this cue is that the smaller the energy difference by flipping the optimal assignment at a site,

Fig. 2.2: CMU-Cornell iCoseg Dataset: Figure shows prototypical images from the co-segmentation groups in our dataset. Note: each image shown above corresponds to a *group* of images.

the more uncertain the system is of its label. We note that min-marginals proposed by [15] could also be used.

2.2.2 Scribble-based Cues

Distance Transform over Scribbles (DT): For this cue, we compute the distance of every pixel to the nearest scribble location. The intuition behind this (weak) cue is that we would like to explore regions in the image away from the current scribble because they hold potentially different features than sites closer to the current scribbles.

Intervening Contours over Scribbles (IC): This cue uses the idea of intervening contours [17]. The value of this cue at each pixel is the maximum edge magnitude in the straight line to the closest scribble. This results in low confusions as we move away from a scribble until a strong edge is observed, and then higher confusions on the other side of the edge. The motivation behind this cue is that edges in images typically denote contrast change, and by observing scribble labels on both sides of an edge, we can learn whether or not to respect such edges for future segmentations.

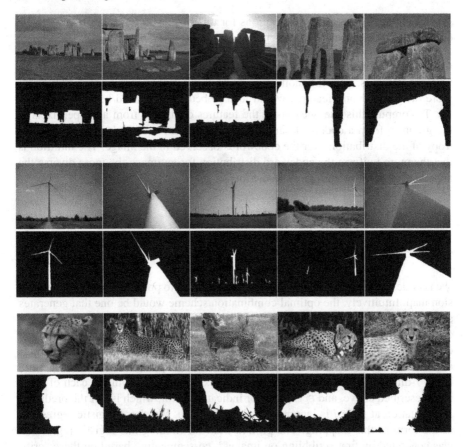

Fig. 2.3: CMU-Cornell iCoseg Dataset: Figure shows the Stonehenge, windmill and cheetah groups. We can see the large variation in illumination, scale, pose and appearance. Masks show the detail in our hand-annotated groundtruth.

2.2.3 Image-level Cues

The cues described so far, are local cues, that describe which region in an image should be scribbled on next. In addition to these, we also use some image-level cues (*i.e.*, uniform over an image), that help predict *which* image to scribble next, not where.

Segment size (SS): We observe that when very few scribbles are marked, energy minimization methods typically over-smooth and results in "whitewash" segmentations (entire image labelled as foreground or background). This cue incorporates a prior for balanced segmentations by assigning higher confusion scores to images with more skewed segmentations. We normalize the size of foreground and background regions to get class distributions for this image, and use the inverse of the entropy of this distribution as our cue.

Codeword Distribution over Images (CD): This image-level cue captures how diverse an image is, with the motivation being that scribbling on images containing more diversity among features would lead to better foreground/background models. To compute this cue, we cluster the features computed from all superpixels in the group to form a codebook, and the confusion score for each image is the entropy of the distribution over the codewords observed in the image. The intuition is that the more uniform the codeword distribution for an image the more diverse the appearances of different regions in the image.

2.2.4 Combined Recommendation Map

We now describe how we combine these various cues to produce a combined confusion map. Intuitively, the optimal combination scheme would be one that generates a recommendation map that assigns high values to regions that a user *would* scribble on, if they were to exhaustively examine all segmentations. Users typically scribble on regions that are incorrectly segmented. We cast the problem of learning the optimal set of weights for our cues as that of learning a mapping $\mathscr{F} : \phi_i \rightarrow \varepsilon_i$, where ϕ_i is the 7-dimensional feature vector for superpixel i, corresponding to each of the 7 cues described above, and ε_i is the error indicator vector, which is 1 if the predicted segmentation at node i is incorrect, and 0 otherwise. We chose logistic regression as the form of this mapping. The ground-truth for training this logistic regression was generated by first scribbling on images[3], co-segmenting based on these scribbles, and then using the mistakes (or the error-map) in these segmentations as the ground-truth. Our cue combination scheme is illustrated in Fig. 2.1.

2.3 The CMU-Cornell iCoseg Dataset

To evaluate our proposed approach and to establish a benchmark for future work, we introduce the largest co-segmentation dataset yet, the CMU-Cornell iCoseg Dataset. While previous works have experimented with a few pairs of images, our dataset contains 38 challenging groups with 643 total images ($\sim$17 images per group), with associated pixel-level ground truth. We built this dataset from the Flickr® online photo collection, and hand-labelled pixel-level segmentations in all images. We used the "Group" feature in Flickr, where users form groups around popular themes, to search for images from this theme. Our dataset consists of animals in the wild

---

[3] More precisely, by generating random automatic scribbles on images. See Section 2.4.1 for details.

(elephants, pandas, *etc.*), popular landmarks (Taj Mahal, Stonehenge, *etc.*), sports teams (Baseball, Football, *etc.*) and other groups that contain a common theme or common foreground object. For some (though not all) of the groups, we restricted the images to come from the same photographer's photo-stream, making this a more realistic scenario. Examples of these groups are shown in various figures in this paper, and Fig. 2.3 shows some prototypical images. We have made this dataset (and annotations) publicly available [2] to facilitate further work, and allow for easy comparisons.

Dataset Annotation: The ground-truth annotations for the dataset were manually generated by a single annotator using a labelling tool. The ground-truth was labelled on superpixels. However, the labelling tool allowed the annotator to interactively obtain finer / coarser superpixels as desired. A useful strategy used by our annotator was to use coarse superpixels while labelling simple scenes, and to use finer superpixels when labelling complicated or cluttered scenes. This allowed for very high quality ground truth, without the labeling task being prohibitively tedious.[4]

	# Groups	# Images	# Images/Group
[22]	7	16	2.29
[13]	23	46	2
CMU-Cornell iCoseg Dataset	**38**	**643**	**16.92**

Table 2.1: Dataset Statistics.

2.3.1 Dataset Statistics

We now analyze some statistics (size, appearance variation, scale variation) of our introduced dataset.

Size: Table 2.1 lists the number of groups, number of images and average number of images per group for our dataset. We note that this dataset is significantly larger than those used in previous works [13, 22]. Fig. 2.5a shows a histogram of number of images in groups.

Appearance: Recall our argument that when consumers take multiple photographs of the same event or object, the images are usually globally consistent. To quantify that images in our dataset do capture this property, we perform the following experiment. Fig. 2.4 shows a pair of images ("girl-pair") from [22], and another

---

[4] Since the superpixels were varied dynamically for each image, they were not the same as the ones used inside our co-segmentation algorithm (which only used a single setting of parameters for generating superpixels in all images).

(a) Girl-pair [22].

(b) Stonehenge-pair from CMU-Cornell iCoseg Dataset.

	KL-Divergence		
	Foreground	Background	Ratio
Girl-pair [22]	1.06	45.78	43.03
Stonehenge-pair	8.49	17.66	2.08

(c) Foreground and background similarity statistics

Fig. 2.4: Appearance Statistics: (a) shows a pair of images ("girl-pair") from [22]; (b) shows a pair of images from the Stonehenge group in our CMU-Cornell iCoseg Dataset; (c) lists the KL-divergences between the two images for each pair. Images in our dataset are globally consistent, with comparable KL-divergence between foregrounds and backgrounds.

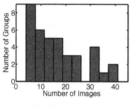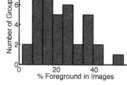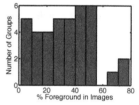

(a) Group Sizes.   (b) Hist. avg. foreground size   (c) largest - smallest foreground

Fig. 2.5: Dataset Statistics: (a) shows the histogram of the number of images in groups; (b) shows histogram of avg. foreground size in groups; (c) shows histogram of difference of largest and smallest foreground object within a group.

pair from our CMU-Cornell iCoseg Dataset ("Stonehenge-pair"). All the foreground pixels from the first pair of images were clustered into 64 color codewords using k-means clustering. A foreground histogram was built over this dictionary for each of the images, and the KL distance was computed between these normalized histograms. Similarly a color dictionary was built using the background pixels and the KL distance between the background distances was computed. This process was repeated for the second pair. We can see that for the "girl-pair" the appearance variation in foreground is considerably smaller than the variation in background. The "Stonehenge-pair", on the other hand, shows a more comparable variation. This is not to say that the CMU-Cornell iCoseg dataset is inherently harder than previous datasets. Our intent is to point out that our dataset contains images where the pre-

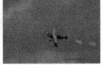

(a) Largest scale-change   (b) Smallest scale-change

Fig. 2.6: Scale Change: (a) shows the largest scale change, and (b) shows the smallest scale change in our dataset.

vious works on co-segmentation would fail, because they have been designed for a different scenario. We hope the introduction of our dataset motivates further research in the problem we consider in this paper.

Scale: To quantify the amount of scale change in our dataset, we show the histogram of average foreground size in groups in Fig. 2.5b. We can see that some groups contain very small foreground objects (on avg. $\leq 5\%$ of the image) while some groups contain very large foreground objects (on avg $\geq 40\%$ of image). In addition, the histogram (Fig. 2.5c) of difference between largest and smallest foreground object in a group shows that even within a group there is significant scale change. Fig. 2.6 shows images with the largest and smallest scale change in our dataset. We can imagine that the large scale changes can be quite challenging for co-segmentation algorithms. In the case of our algorithm however, scale changes should not matter too much.

2.4 Experiments

For experimental evaluation, we performed machine experiments (Section 2.4.1) by generating synthetic scribbles, and also performed user-study (Section 2.4.2). In all experiments in this paper, we quantify the accuracy of an image segmentation as the percentage of pixels whose labels are correctly predicted. Co-segmentation accuracy for a group is the average segmentation accuracy over all images in this group.

2.4.1 Machine Experiments

To conduct a thorough set of experiments and evaluate various design choices, it is important to be able to perform multiple iterations without explicitly polling a human for scribbles. Thus, we develop a mechanism to generate automatic scribbles, that mimic human scribbles. We model the scribbles as (smooth) random walks that do not cross foreground-background boundaries. Our scribble generation technique consists of sampling a starting point in the image uniformly at random. A direction

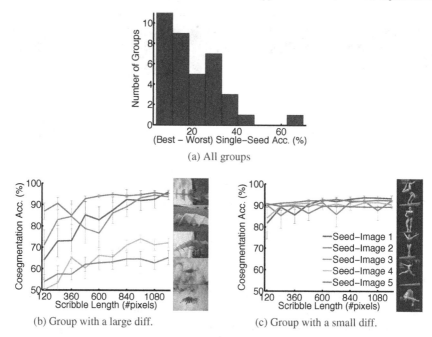

(a) All groups

(b) Group with a large diff. (c) Group with a small diff.

Fig. 2.7: Diversity within a group: (a) histogram of the difference in accuracy between the best and worst seed-images for all the groups in our dataset. A large difference indicates diversity in appearance. Some groups such as (b) "Kite" have images with varied appearances (two images providing worst segmentation accuracies don't contain any grass), while other groups such as (c) "Gymnast" are more homogenous. Best viewed in colour.

angle is then randomly sampled such that it is highly correlated with the previous direction sample (for smoothness) for the scribble,[5] and a fixed-size (=30 pixels) step is taken along this direction to extend the scribble (as long as it does not cross object boundaries, as indicated by the groundtruth segmentation of the image). To mimic user-scribbles given a recommendation map, the initial as well as subsequent points on the scribble are picked by considering the recommendation map to be a distribution. Using synthetic scribbles allows us to control the length of scribbles and observe the behavior of the algorithm with increasing information. Example synthetic scribbles are shown in Fig. 2.9. For all experiments in this paper, the length of each individual scribble was capped at 120 pixels.

---

[5] For the first two sampled points, there is no previous direction and this direction is sampled uniformly at random.

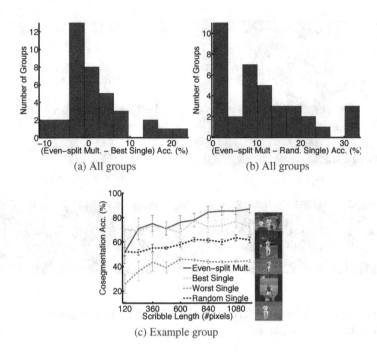

(a) All groups   (b) All groups

(c) Example group

Fig. 2.8: Sparse vs. Dense Scribbles: (a) and (b) show the histograms of accuracy gains of even-split over the best (single) seed-image and a random (single) seed-image, respectively; (c) compares the accuracies achieved by dense scribbles on a single image, and sparse scribbles on multiple images for the group shown. Again, images are ordered in decreasing accuracy. The second histogram (b) shows providing scribbles on multiple images is a better strategy than committing to a single one.

2.4.1.1 Baseline 1: Scribbles restricted to a Single Image

To establish the simplest baseline, we ask the following question: "how well would interactive co-segmentation work if we were restricted to scribbling on a single image?" If a group consisted of successive frames from a video sequence, the choice of this chosen image (seed-image) would not matter much. The higher the diversity in the images among a group, the more variation we would observe in the group segmentation accuracies achieved by various seed-images, because not all seed-images would provide useful statistics for the group as a whole. We use the synthetically generated scribbles (described above) to test this.

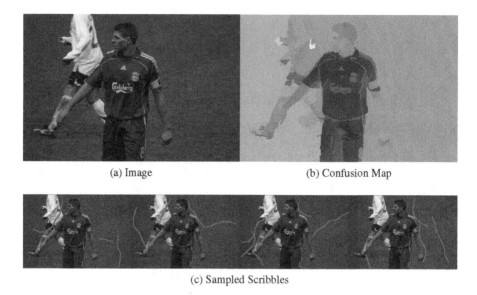

(a) Image   (b) Confusion Map

(c) Sampled Scribbles

Fig. 2.9: Example simulated scribbles: Note that these scribbles never cross fore-ground boundaries (red player).

In Fig. 2.7a we show the histogram of the difference in accuracy between the best and worst seed-images for all the groups in our dataset.[6] We can see that the histogram has a heavy tail, with 28 (of 37) groups having greater than 10% differ-ence (and one as high as 69%), indicating that most groups have a lot of variation. Figs. 2.7b and 2.7c show the co-segmentation accuracies (Y-axis) for the "kite" and "gymnast" group respectively, as a function of the total length of scribbles (X-axis) on different seed-images in these groups (shown next to them). Images are ordered in decreasing accuracy. The "Kite" groups is an example of the groups with a lot of variation while the images in the "Gymnast" group have similar performances. Notice that in the "Kite" group, the two "bad" images do not contain any grass, and thus irrespective of the length of the scribbles on them, the algorithm will not know whether grass is considered foreground or background, and thus the group co-segmentation accuracy does not rise above 75%.

2.4.1.2 Aside: Automatic Seed Image Selection:

Before we describe the second baseline that we compare our interactive co-segmentation approach to, we take a small detour related to the previous baseline. Clearly, if we

---

[6] In order to keep statistics comparable across groups, we select a random subset of 5 images from all groups in our dataset. One of our groups consisted of 4 images only, so all our results are reported on 37 groups.

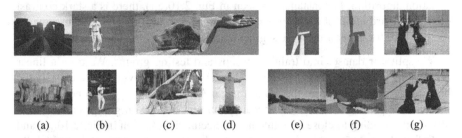

(a)　　　(b)　　　(c)　　　(d)　　　(e)　　　(f)　　　(g)

Fig. 2.10: For columns (a-e), top and bottom rows show best and worst images from example groups, which motivate our choice of features (a) Illumination histogram (b) HSV colour histogram (c) Gradient histogram (d) Gist and (e) Segmentation histogram; (f) Segmentations of images shown in (e); (g) Two images from the group are very similar with similar segmentation accuracies making the ranking a slightly misleading metric.

were restricted to scribble on only one image in a group, the choice of the seed image is crucial. This naturally leads to the question "Given a group of images to be co-segmented by scribbling on one image, can we automatically select this seed image in an intelligent way?".

We pose this seed image selection problem as a classification task [4]. We extract the following features to describe an image.

- Illumination histogram: One of the observations we made was that the presence of strong shadows across the image (Fig. 2.10(a)) often results in poor co-segmentation accuracies. To capture this intuition, we compute a 50-dim histogram of the gray scale image.
- Hue, Saturation and Value entropy: The variety of colours in an image typically corresponds to the amount of useful information in the image, as seen in Fig. 2.10(b). We quantify this via a 3-dim vector holding the entropies of the hue, saturation and value marginal histograms. The more the number of colours present in an image, the higher the entropies in these distributions would be.
- Gradient histogram: The distribution of the strength of edges is a good indicator of how interesting the image is in terms of the existence of several regions/objects in the image. To represent this, we compute a 20-dim histogram of the edge magnitudes across the image. Fig. 2.10(c) shows that the worst image in the group has very few strong edges as compared to the best image which has more variety in its content.
- Scene Gist: The Gist features can help capture a holistic view of the overall scene layout (Fig. 2.10(d)) . We extract the 1280-dim Gist features [20] which captures the response of the image to gabor filters of different orientations and scales, along with the spatial layout of these responses over the image.
- Segmentation histogram: Another indicator of the scene layout is the distribution of the sizes of segments in an image when run through an off-the-shelf segmen-

tation algorithm. For instance, as seen in Fig. 2.10(e,f), there is a stark contrast in the distribution of sizes of segments found in these images. We use mean-shift [10] for generating these segmentations.

We split our dataset into training groups and testing groups. We train a linear SVM using each of the n_f (=5) features described above individually to classify the best image in a group from the worst image. At training time we do not consider the remaining images in a group, because multiple images in groups can be visually similar leading to close cosegmentation accuracies, as seen in Fig. 2.10(g), and including them during training would make the classification problem artificially hard.

During testing, each image from the test group is passed through these n_f SVMs, and their output scores are recorded. Let the score corresponding to image x_i and SVM (feature) f_a be μ_i^a. The best images in training groups were labeled as the positive class, and thus we expect μ_i^a to be higher for better images.

We are ultimately interested in a ranking of the m images in the test group, and in order to do so, we compute a quality measure for each image, by comparing it to every other image in the group. Each image x_i is assigned a quality measure

$$Q(x_i) = \sum_{j=1}^{m} \sum_{a=1}^{n_f} [\![(\mu_i^a - \mu_j^a)]\!] \tag{2.3}$$

where $[\![t]\!]$ is the sign function, i.e. $+1$ if $t > 0$, and -1 otherwise.

This effectively captures how many times the image x_i got voted as being better than other images in the group, among all features. The m images in a group are ranked by this measure, and the top ranked image is chosen as the seed image.

For our experiments, we select m to be 5, and retain a random subset of 5 images from all groups. Since one of the 38 groups contained only 4 images, we work with the remaining 37 groups. We perform leave-one-out cross-validation on the groups. To understand the effectiveness of each of the individual features, we first report their corresponding image classification accuracies for identifying the best image from the worst. The results are shown in Fig. 2.11. It can be seen that all features hold some information to identify the best images from the worst ones (significantly outperforming chance, which would be 50%). It can be seen that the HSV entropies have the highest accuracy ($\sim$92%). This is understandable, especially since the segmentation algorithm uses colour features. All other features have similar accuracies ($\sim$76%).

To quantify the quality of the final ranking determined by our approach, we match our predicted ranks of images in the test groups, to the ground truth ranks (determined by sorting the average cosegmentation accuracies). We find that on average (across groups), we assign a rank of 2.14 to images that have a ground truth rank of 1. Moreover, the images that we select as rank 1, have, on average, a ground-truth rank of 2.11. In both cases, a random classifier would have an average rank of 3. Although this improvement in ranks may not seem significant, it should be noted that often groups contain more than one image that are "good" for scribbling and give similar segmentation accuracies, e.g. images shown in in Fig. 2.10(g).

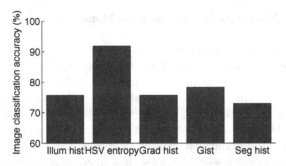

Fig. 2.11: The classification accuracies of each of our features in identifying best images in a group from the worst images.

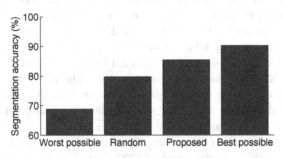

Fig. 2.12: The final cosegmentation accuracies.

The most relevant metric, for our application, is the gain in cosegmentation accuracies achieved by using our proposed seed image selection algorithm, as compared to picking an image from the group at random, which is the heuristic used by previous works [12, 24]. These results are shown in Fig. 2.12. We see that there is more than a 10% gap in the cosegmentation accuracies that can be achieved by scribbling on a randomly selected image (79.7%), and picking the best image in each group (90.2%). It should be noted that the best accuracy is the accuracy which would be achieved if an oracle were to label the best image in each group, and hence is the upper bound on what accuracy we can achieve. We can see that by scribbling on an image recommended by the seed image selection algorithm, we can fill more than half of this gap (at 85.4%).

Of course, the question of automatic seed image selection, while an interesting thought exercise, is relevant only if the user is restricted to scribbling on a single image in a group. As described thus far, our interactive co-segmentation system is more general, and recommends meaningful regions across all images in the group to the user to provide scribbles on. After this brief side analysis, we now focus again on the second baseline that we compare our approach to.

2.4.1.3 Baseline 2: Uniform Recommendation Maps

In the previous baseline we were restricted to scribbling on a single image. As we saw, the performance between the best and the worst seed-images could be significantly different. In this section, we consider user scribbles to be a limited resource and evaluate whether it is better to seek sparse scribbles on multiple images or dense scribbles on a single image. We follow a similar setup as in the last section, only now the scribbles are evenly split across all images in the group, which corresponds to uniform recommendation maps on all images. This way we can compare 1200-pixel scribbles (which would be dense) in a single image with five 240-pixel scribbles (which would be sparse).[7] In practice, instead of making one long 1200-pixel scribble, we sample scribbles of length at most 120 pixels, and evenly split scribbles between foreground and background. As before, we perform 10 random runs. Fig. 2.8c shows the average cosegmentation accuracies in the group (Y-axis) for the worst (single) seed-image, the best (single) seed-image, a random (single) seed-image, and the accuracy achieved by evenly splitting scribbles across all images (called even-split) as a function of the total length of scribbles (X-axis). We can see that for the same length of scribbles, evenly splitting them across all images in the group and getting sparse scribbles performs better than dense scribbles on any image in this group. Fig. 2.8a and 2.8b show the histogram of accuracy gains of even-split over the best (single) seed-image and the random (single) seed-image experiments over all of the groups. The accuracies for Figs 2.8a,2.8b were computed using scribbles of total length of 1200 pixels, *i.e.*, they correspond to the rightmost datapoint in Fig.2.8c. We can see while even-split performs better than the best (single) seed-image for most groups, it is strictly better than a random (single) seed-image for *all* of the groups.

2.4.1.4 iCoseg

We first analyze the informativeness of each of our 7 cues. We start by generating a foreground and background scribble each of length at most 120 pixels on a random image in a group. We then compute each of our cues, and treat each individual cue as a recommendation map. We generate the next synthetic scribble (again of at most 120 pixels) as guided by this recommendation map, meaning that points are sampled by treating this recommendation map as a probability distribution (instead of sampling them randomly). We repeat this till we have scribbled about 1200 pixels across the group, and compute the average segmentation accuracy across the images of a group. We rank the 7 cues by this accuracy. Fig. 2.14 shows the mean ranks (across groups, average of 10 random runs) achieved by these cues. Out of our cues, the graph-cut cue (GC) performs the best, while both distance transform (DT) and intervening contour (IC) are the weakest. GC cue quantifies the uncertainty of the entire model (including node and edge potentials) and thus is expected to provide

---

[7] This is one of the reasons for keeping a constant number of images per group. If each group had different images, even-split performance would no longer be comparable across groups.

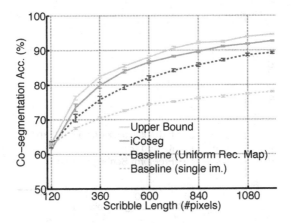

Fig. 2.13: Machine Experiments: Figure shows average co-segmentation accuracy as a function of the number of scribbles (each scribble is 120 pixels). iCoseg significantly outperforms baselines and is close to a natural upper-bound (see Section 2.4.1 for details).

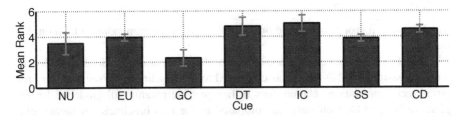

Fig. 2.14: Mean ranks achieved by individual cues (see Sec 2.4.1).

the best indication of where more information is required (from an active learning perspective). Thus, it is not surprising that this cue performs the best. DT and IC on the other hand completely ignore the learnt model, and only consider low-level cues like where (in x,y co-ordinates) we have scribbled in the image so far and the gradients in the image which often do not coincide with object boundaries. Thus, it is not surprising that they provide the least information to recommend meaningful regions to scribble further on.

We now evaluate iCoseg, our recommendation system, as a whole. The experimental set up is the same as that described above, except now we use the combined recommendation map to guide subsequent scribbles (and not individual cues). The cue combination weights are learnt from all groups except one that we test on (leave-one-out cross validation). We compare to two baselines described above. One is that of using a uniform recommendation map on all images in the group, which essentially means randomly scribbling on the images (respecting object boundaries of course). And the other (even weaker) baseline is that of selecting only one image

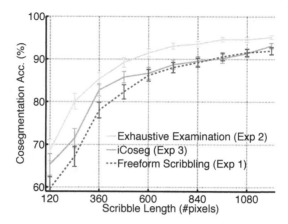

Fig. 2.15: User Study: Average performance of subjects in the three conducted experiments (see Section 2.4.2). iCoseg (Exp. 3) requires significantly less effort for users, and allows them to reach 80% co-seg accuracy with 75% the effort of Exp. 1.

(randomly) in a group to scribble on (with a uniform recommendation map on this image).

Fig. 2.13 shows the performance of our combined recommendation map (iCoseg) with increasing scribble length, as compared to the baselines. We see that our proposed recommendation scheme does in fact provide meaningful guidance for regions to be scribbled on next (as compared to the two baselines). A meaningful upper-bound would be the segmentation accuracy that could be achieved if an oracle told us where the segmentations were incorrect, and subsequent scribbles were provided only in these erroneous regions. As seen in Fig. 2.13, iCoseg performs very close to this upper bound, which means that users following our recommendations can achieve cutout performances comparable to those achieved by analyzing mistakes in all cutouts with significantly less effort *without* ever having to examine all cutouts explicitly.

2.4.2 User Study

In order to further test iCoseg, we developed a java-based user-interface for interactive co-segmentation.[8] We conducted a user study to verify our hypothesis that our proposed approach can help *real* users produce good quality cutouts from a group of images, without needing to exhaustively examine mistakes in all images at each iteration. Our study involved 15 participants performing 3 experiments (each involving

---

[8] We believe this interface may be useful to other researchers working on interactive applications and we have made it publicly available [2].

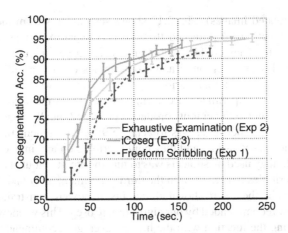

Fig. 2.16: User Study: Average performance of subjects in the three conducted experiments as a function of time (see Section 2.4.2). We can see that for a fixed amount of time, iCoseg (Exp. 3) typically achieves highest co-segmentation accuracy.

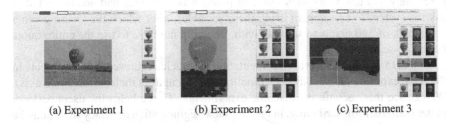

(a) Experiment 1   (b) Experiment 2   (c) Experiment 3

Fig. 2.17: User Study Screenshots: (a) Exp. 1: subjects were not shown cutouts and were free to scribble on any image/region while respecting the foreground/background boundaries; (b) Exp. 2: subjects exhaustively examine all segmentations and scribble on mistakes (cyan indicates foreground); (c) Exp. 3: users were instructed to scribble in the region recommended by iCoseg. Best viewed in colour.

	Mean no. of fg/bg scribbles per iter	Mean length of scribbles (px)	Mean % fg. in scribbles	Amount of uncertainty under the scribbles
Machine experiments	1.00 / 1.00	120	23%	-
User studies				
Exp. 1	1.04 / 1.05	106	46%	0.49 ± 0.04
Exp. 2	1.07 / 1.07	110	-	0.49 ± 0.04
Exp. 3	1.05 / 1.06	99	-	0.53 ± 0.04

Table 2.2: Comparison between user study and machine experiments.

5 groups of 5 related images). Fig. 2.17 shows screen-shots from the three experiments. The subjects were informed that the first experiment was to acclimatize them to the system. They could scribble anywhere on any image, as long as they used blue scribbles on foreground and red scribbles on background. The system computed cutouts based on their scribbles, but the subjects were never shown these cutouts. We call this experiment "freeform-scribbling". In the second experiment, the subjects were shown the cutouts produced produced on all images in the group from their scribbles. Their goal was to achieve 95% co-segmentation accuracy in as few interactions as possible, and they could scribble on any image. We observed that a typical strategy used by subjects was to find the worst cutout at every iteration, and then add scribbles to correct it. In the third experiment, they had the same goal, but this time, while they were shown all cutouts, they were constrained to scribble within a window recommended by our algorithm, iCoseg. This window position was chosen by finding the location with the highest average recommendation value (in the combined recommendation map) in a neighbourhood of 201×201 pixels. The use of a window was merely to make the user-interface intuitive, and other choices could be explored. In all three experiments, users were restricted to use only 120 pixels of scribbles per iteration. Our UI displayed a counter that showed how many pixels they had left. Once their quota of pixels was over, they had no choice but to ask the system to co-segment using these scribbles, after which they were given a new quota of 120 pixels to scribble with. They did not have to use the entire quota before co-segmenting.

Fig. 2.15 shows the average segmentation accuracies achieved by the subjects in the three experiments (Y-axis) as a function of the length of their scribbles (X-axis). We can see that, as with the machine experiments, iCoseg helps the users perform better than freeform scribbling, in that the same segmentation accuracy (83%) can be achieved with about 75% the effort. In addition, the average time taken by the users for one iteration of scribbling reduced from 20.2 seconds (exhaustively examining all cutouts) to 14.2 seconds (iCoseg), an average saving of 60 seconds per group. Thus, our approach enables users to achieve cutout accuracies comparable to those achieved by analyzing mistakes in all cutouts, in significantly less time. This fact is further shown in Fig. 2.16 where the co-segmentation accuracy achieved (Y-axis) is plotted as a function of time taken (X-axis) for each of the three expirments, averaged across users and groups. We can see that our approach allows users to reach highest accuracies given the same time budget.

2.4.3 Comparing Machine Experiments and User Study

In order to understand how users scribbled in our user-study and study how well our automatic scribbles (machine experiments) emulate this, we analyze similarities between the user and synthetic scribbles. Table 2.2 compares some statistics.

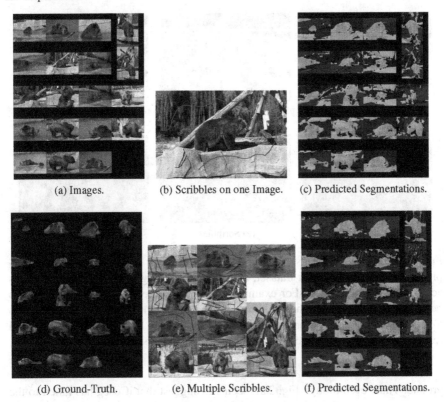

(a) Images. (b) Scribbles on one Image. (c) Predicted Segmentations.

(d) Ground-Truth. (e) Multiple Scribbles. (f) Predicted Segmentations.

Fig. 2.18: Common Failure Case: (a) shows the group of images; (c) shows the segmentations achieved by scribbling on a single image, shown in (b). Cyan indicates foreground. (f) shows the segmentations achieved by scribbles on multiple images, shown in (e). When foreground and background have a lot of overlap in colour distributions, our interactive segmentation method faces difficulty in producing accurate segmentations (compare segmentations in (c),(f) with ground-truth in (d)). However, our algorithms allows for straightforward incorporation of more sophisticated features (*e.g.* colour-pallet of [12]), which should result in better performance.

Our automatic scribbles were generated for foreground and background with a fixed length of 120 pixels, and we see that they are comparable to the user scribbles in both the length and the average number of scribbles.

Interestingly, we also found that while our subjects were not given an explicit goal in Exp. 1 (freeform scribbling experiment) and were not shown the groundtruth, they were implicitly aware of the common foreground and their scribbles reflected that knowledge. The proportion of foreground pixels in all scribbles given by our subjects (for Exp. 1) was 46%, while the groups they viewed only contained 23% foreground. Clearly, they weren't scribbling uniformly randomly over an image, but were dividing their scribbles somewhat evenly over the foreground and back-

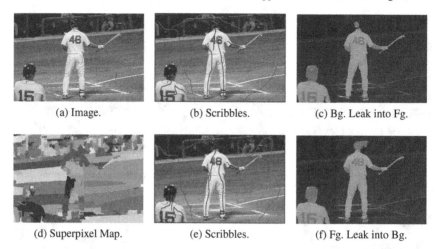

| (a) Image. | (b) Scribbles. | (c) Bg. Leak into Fg. |

| (d) Superpixel Map. | (e) Scribbles. | (f) Fg. Leak into Bg. |

Fig. 2.19: Superpixel Leaks: We use a single parameter setting to generate super-pixels for all images in our dataset, and thus some images show superpixel leaks across foreground objects. For example, in (d), the superpixel on the head of the baseball player leaks into the background. As a result, the segmentation also tends to either leak from foreground to background (f), or from background to foreground (c), depending on the choice of scribbles, (e) and (b) respectively.

ground. Thus, even though Fig. 2.15 seems to suggest that iCoseg has fallen to the performance level of the freeform-scribble baseline (Exp. 1), in reality, "freeform scribbling" has become a smart human-attention based algorithm. The truly random baseline can be seen in Fig. 2.13 where we force the random scribbles to be truly uniformly random, which our algorithm easily outperforms.

We also measured whether users were scribbling on confusing areas, as measured by our combined uncertainty map (which is normalized to be a spatial probability distribution, and thus between 0 and 1). We notice that the amount of uncertainty under user-scribbles is 0.49 ± 0.04 for both Exp. 1 (freeform scribbling) and Exp. 2 (exhaustive examination), again indicating that the users were implicitly aware about the common foreground and scribbled over incorrect segmentations which are typically regions with high uncertainty. We note that the uncertainty under user scribbles increased to 0.53 ± 0.04 for Exp. 3 (iCoseg), which is understandable, because the users were guided to scribble within the indicated regions of high un-certainty.

2.4.4 Limitations and Failure Cases

An assumption of our approach is that the foreground and background models are different enough in the chosen feature space (*i.e.* colour for our experiments) to allow for reliable labelling of both classes. The interactive nature of our system makes the choice of features and appearance models seem less critical. However, they play an important role, and it is important to analyze the limitations and failure cases of our approach.

Non-discriminative Features: The most common failure case for our method results from the choice of colour features. Fig. 2.18 shows a difficult group to segment because the foreground colour distribution is very similar to the background colour distribution. Thus, even though the scribble guidance leads users to useful locations, the co-segmentation quality does not significantly improve despite multiple rounds of scribbles. Figs. 2.18b,c show the co-segmentations after scribbling on a single image, and Figs. 2.18e,f show the co-segmentations after scribbling on multiple images. We note that the choice of colour features is not inherent to the system, and more sophisticated features can be seamlessly incorporated. One choice of better features would be color-pattern features of [12] that capture the spatial distribution of colors in a neighborhood. These would provide more discriminative power (which should result in improved performance), as well as help overcome the the local nature of features extracted at superpixels.

Superpixel leaks: We use superpixels as the labelling sites in our framework. This speeds up our implementation because the graph constructed on superpixels is significantly smaller than the grid-graph on pixels. However, because we use a single parameter setting to generate superpixels for all images in our dataset, some images show superpixel leaks across foreground objects. Fig. 2.19 shows an example image. Notice that some superpixels leak across object boundaries, *e.g.*, the one on the head of the baseball player. As a result of this superpixel leak, the segmentation also tends to either leak from foreground to background or from background to foreground, depending on the choice of scribbles. Having said this, our approach can be trivially extended to work with pixels, for applications that require highly accurate segmentations.

Single Background Model: It is conceivable that the use of multiple background models within a group could be beneficial. However, the more models we wish to build, the more scribbles we are likely to need from users for the models to be informative. In the extreme, in order to have one background model for every image in the group, we would need sufficient scribbles in all images in the group. This, to some extent, would defeat the purpose of having a co-segmentation system, where the goal is to leverage the fact that topically-related images share foreground and background statistics, and hence can be co-segmented, and need not be segmented individually. As seen in our examples, a large proportion of the images within a group do share similar backgrounds, a property that should be exploited when possible, but these properties are of course, application dependent.

In order to quantify the above intuition, we performed the following experiment. We performed co-segmentation with synthetic scribbles for the following three cases:

- Multiple Models, Independent Segmentation (MMIS). In this case, the synthetic user scribbles on each of the five images in a group, and each image is independently segmented. Intuitively, this is equivalent to running a standard Grab-cut-like method on each image in the group, thus forcing the user to scribble on all images. The appearance models are not shared and the user is forced to scribble on all images to be segmented.
- Multiple Models, Co-Segmentation (MMCS). In this case, the synthetic user again scribbles on a single image in the group, however now all images in the group are segmented by sharing the appearance model learnt from the single scribbled image. This is repeated by scribbling on all images in the group one at a time. As we have already observed in Section 2.4.1.3 and Fig. 2.8, we do not expect this combination to perform well.
- Single Model, Co-Segmentation (SMCS). This is the case described in our machine experiments (Section 2.4.1 and Fig. 2.13), where the synthetic user scribbles on all images in the group. All images in the group are segmented by sharing the appearance model learnt from all the scribbled images.

	MMIS	MMCS	SMCS
Segmentation Accuracy	97.07 %	79.71 %	92.67 %

Table 2.3: Segmentation accuracies for various setups averaged across groups.

As we can see in Table 2.3, MMIS is the best thing to do, *i.e.* to scribble on every image and segment all images independently. However, this requires users to scribble on all images, which is not feasible for scenarios where the group contains many images. On the other hand, SMCS relieves the user from this constraint of scribbling on all images and as our machine experiments and user study show, the savings provided by iCoseg are crucial.

Now that we have presented a detailed description of iCoseg which allows users to interactively co-segment an object of interest from a group of images, in the following chapter, we discuss various exciting applications that are enabled by such a co-segmentation tool.

References

1. Bagon, S.: Matlab Wrapper for Graph Cut. http://www.wisdom.weizmann.ac.il/~bagon (2006).
2. Batra, D., Kowdle, A., Parikh, D., Tang, K., Chen, T.: Interactive Cosegmentation by Touch. http://amp.ece.cornell.edu/projects/touch-coseg/ (2009).
3. Batra, D., Kowdle, A., Parikh, D., Luo, J., Chen, T.: Interactively Co-segmentating Topically Related Images with Intelligent Scribble Guidance. International Journal of Computer Vision (2011).

4. Batra, D., Parikh, D., Kowdle, A., Chen, T., Luo, J.: Seed Image Selection in Interactive Coseg-mentation. International Conference on Image Processing (2009).
5. Batra, D., Sukthankar, R., Chen, T.: Semi-Supervised Clustering via Learnt Codeword Dis-tances. British Machine Vision Conference (2008).
6. Bouman, C.A.: Cluster: An unsupervised algorithm for modeling Gaussian mixtures. Avail-able from http://www.ece.purdue.edu/\string~bouman. (1997).
7. Boykov, Y.Y., Jolly, M.-P.: Interactive graph cuts for optimal boundary and region segmenta-tion of objects in N-D images. International Conference on Computer Vision (2001).
8. Boykov, Y., Kolmogorov, V.: An Experimental Comparison of Min-Cut/Max-Flow Algorithms for Energy Minimization in Vision. IEEE Transactions on Pattern Analysis and Machine In-telligence (2004).
9. Boykov, Y., Veksler, O., Zabih, R.: Efficient Approximate Energy Minimization via Graph Cuts. IEEE Transactions on Pattern Analysis and Machine Intelligence (2001).
10. Comaniciu, D., Meer, P.: Mean shift: a robust approach toward feature space analysis. IEEE Transactions on Pattern Analysis and Machine Intelligence (2002).
11. Criminisi, A., Sharp, T., Blake, A.: GeoS: Geodesic Image Segmentation. European Confer-ence on Computer Vision (2008).
12. Cui, J., Yang, Q., Wen, F., Wu, Q., Zhang, C,. Gool, L.V., Tang, T.: Transductive Object Cutout. IEEE Conference on Computer Vision and Pattern Recognition (2008).
13. Hochbaum, D.S., Singh, V.: An efficient algorithm for co-segmentation. International Confer-ence on Computer Vision (2009).
14. Hoiem, D., Efros, A.A., Hebert, M.: Geometric context from a single image. International Conference on Computer Vision (2005).
15. Kohli, P., Philip, T.H,S: Measuring uncertainty in graph cut solutions. Elsevier Journal on Computer Vision and Image Understanding (2008).
16. Kolmogorov, V., Zabih, R.: What Energy Functions can be Minimized via Graph Cuts?. IEEE Transactions on Pattern Analysis and Machine Intelligence (2004).
17. Leung, T., Malik, J.: Contour continuity in region based image segmentation. European Con-ference on Computer Vision (1998).
18. Mu, Y.D., Zhou, B.F.: Co-segmentation of Image Pairs with Quadratic Global Constraint in MRFs. Asian Conference on Computer Vision (2007).
19. Mukherjee, L., Singh, V., Dyer, C.R.: Half-integrality based algorithms for cosegmentation of images. IEEE Conference on Computer Vision and Pattern Recognition (2009).
20. Oliva, A., Torralba, A.: Modeling the Shape of the Scene: A Holistic Representation of the Spatial Envelope. International Journal of Computer Vision (2001).
21. Rother, C., Kolmogorov, V., Blake, A.: GrabCut: interactive foreground extraction using iter-ated graph cuts. ACM Transactions on Graphics (Proceedings of SIGGRAPH) (2004).
22. Rother, C., Minka, T., Blake, A., Kolmogorov, V., Cosegmentation of Image Pairs by His-togram Matching - Incorporating a Global Constraint into MRFs (2006)
23. Seung, H.S., Opper, M., Sompolinsky, H.: Query by committee. Computational Learning The-ory (1992).
24. Schnitman, Y., Caspi, Y., Cohen O.D.. Lischinski, D.: Inducing Semantic Segmentation from an Example. Asian Conference on Computer Vision (2006).

Chapter 3
Applications

Abstract The task of segmenting out the foreground from a group of topically related images lends itself to a number of interesting applications. One such application is creating a photo collage. We can imagine a scenario where a user captures a set of photographs of an object of interest, and would like to segment the object out from the cluttered background to make a collage out of the cutouts. An extension to this would include overlaying the foreground cutouts on a novel background without the need for the traditional green room studio setting. As we show in this chapter, interactive co-segmentation allows for an easy way to achieve these using simple strokes even in the presence of cluttered backgrounds. Moreover, recent work has shown that interactive co-segmentation can be extended to image based modeling applications, specifically obtaining a 3D model of an object of interest just from a collection of images of this object. Finally, we show that interactive co-segmentation can be extended beyond object co-segmentation – the same techniques can be applied to 3D surfaces in a scene to obtain a dense piecewise planar model of the scene captured from multiple viewpoints.

3.1 Photo Collage

The task of segmenting out the foreground from a group of topically related images lends itself to a number of interesting applications. One such application is creating a photo collage. We can imagine a scenario where we capture a set of photographs of our pet, or our favorite baseball team, and we would like to extract out the common foreground from the cluttered background to make a collage out of the cutouts.

One approach to achieve this is to use single image interactive segmentation on each image in our group of images, thus extracting out the foreground. However, this can be very tedious and time consuming. As the number of images in our group increases the amount of user effort needed increases rapidly. The interactive co-segmentation algorithm introduced in Chapter 2, iCoseg, makes this task significantly easier. Consider for example the group of images shown in Fig. 3.1. Images like these are fairly representative of a typical consumer photo collection. Using iCoseg, a user can extract out the foreground across all the images, by providing simple scribbles, and create a collage.

One can provide enough control to the user to perform some basic manipulations on the cutouts such as scaling, translation and rotation to create a novel photo collage of choice. Fig. 3.2 provides one such example.

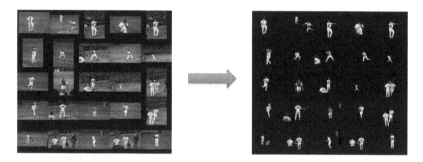

Fig. 3.1: Photo Collage: Interactive co-segmentation allows the user to cut-out the common foreground, in this case the Red Sox players and create a collage using the cutouts. (Best viewed in color).

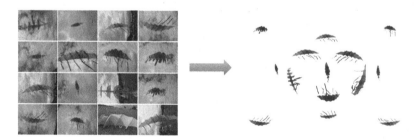

Fig. 3.2: Photo Collage: Interactive co-segmentation allows the user to cut-out the common foreground, the kite from a kite festival and build a creative photo collage using the cutouts. (Best viewed in color).

3.2 Object-of-Interest 3D Modeling

The past decade has seen an exponential growth in the popularity of immersive virtual environments (like Second-Life®with 6.1 Million members) and gaming envi-

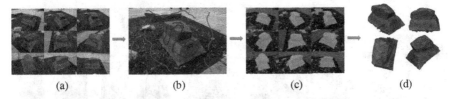

Fig. 3.3: Object-of-Interest 3D Modeling: (a) Stone dataset (24 images) - subset of images given to the system shown; (b) User interactions to indicate the object of interest (blue scribbles = object of interest, red scribbles = background); (c) Resulting silhouettes after co-segmentation (object of interest in cyan color) (d) Some sample novel views of the rendered 3D model (Best viewed in color).

ronments (like Microsoft Xbox Kinect®). Accompanying this growth has been the need for personalization and intelligent augmentation. For example, gamers want to be able to "scan" and use their own gear (like skateboards) in a skateboarding game. The computer-vision task then is to create a 3D model of this object of interest from a collection of images of this object.

One approach to achieve this, would be to haul an expensive laser scanner to get precise depth estimates in a controlled setup, and reconstruct the object [16]. However, this might not be a feasible solution for average users. Another typical approach is to capture images of the object in a controlled environment like a multi-camera studio with mono-color screen [1, 3, 6, 8, 22, 24] or structured lighting [25], and then use something like a shape-from-silhouette algorithm [2, 5, 7, 23] to construct the 3D model. Although these techniques have produced promising results in these constrained settings, this is a tedious process, and in some cases not an option (for example, immovable objects like a statue, historically or culturally-significant artifacts). Moreover, general scene reconstruction algorithms are not designed to focus on the object of interest to the user.

Fig. 3.4: Dino dataset (36 images): (a) Subset of the collection of images given to the system where the dino was marked as the object of interest; (b) Resulting silhouettes after co-segmentation (in cyan color); (c) Some sample novel views of the 3D model (Best viewed in color).

(a)   (b)   (c)

Fig. 3.5: Statue dataset (38 images): (a) Subset of the collection of images given
to the system where the statue was marked as the object of interest; (b) Resulting
silhouettes after co-segmentation (in cyan color); (c) Some sample novel views of
the 3D model (Best viewed in color).

(a)   (b)   (c)

Fig. 3.6: Clock tower dataset (32 images): (a) Subset of the collection of images
given to the system where the clock tower was marked as the object of interest; (b)
Resulting silhouettes after co-segmentation (in cyan color); (c) Some sample novel
views of the 3D model (Best viewed in color).

Co-segmentation can come to the rescue. We first interactively co-segment the
object of interest in the group of images using iCoseg. We then use the structure-
from-motion implementation by [21] called 'Bundler' to recover camera parameters for each image in this group. Using the silhouettes from iCoseg, and camera
parameters obtained from structure-from-motion [21], in conjunction with a octree-
reconstruction-based shape-from-silhouette algorithm [2, 23] we generate a texture
mapped 3D model of the object of interest. Fig. 3.3 shows an overview of the algorithm. For more details the reader is referred to [13].

Results. Figs. 3.4,3.7,3.6,3.5,3.8,3.9 show results on a number of datasets ranging
from a simple collection taken in a controlled setup to a community photo collection
and a video captured in a cluttered scene. In each figure, we show the rendered 3D
model for each dataset, captured from novel view-points. For all datasets except the
dino dataset, we texture map the model by back-projecting the faces of the mesh
onto a single image.

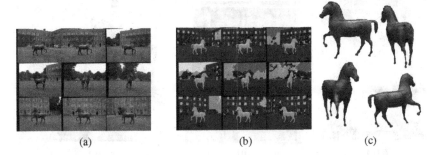

(a)   (b)   (c)

Fig. 3.7: Cambridge unicorn dataset (14 images): (a) Subset of the collection of images given to the system where the unicorn statue was marked as the object of interest; (b) Resulting silhouettes after co-segmentation (in cyan color); (c) Some sample novel views of the 3D model (Best viewed in color).

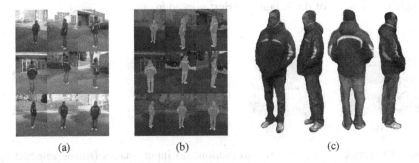

(a)   (b)   (c)

Fig. 3.8: Video dataset (17 images obtained by sampling the video): (a) Subset of the collection of images given to the system where the person was considered the object of interest; (b) Resulting silhouettes after co-segmentation; (c) Some sample novel views of the 3D model (Best viewed in color).

3.3 Scribble based 3D reconstruction of scenes via scene co-segmentation

In this section, we show that interactive co-segmentation can be extended beyond co-segmentating objects – the same techniques can be applied to 3D surfaces in a scene to obtain a dense piecewise planar model of the scene captured from multiple viewpoints. We review our previous work [14].

The goal is to obtain a visually pleasing reconstruction of the scene. First, we extend interactive co-segmentation from a binary (foreground-background) problem to a multi-label problem. Next, we develop a novel scribble-based interactive 3D-reconstruction algorithm where simple interactions from the user indicating the

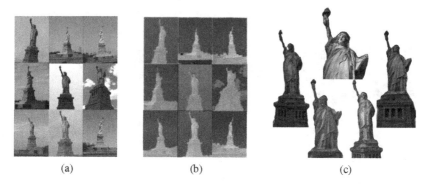

(a)   (b)   (c)

Fig. 3.9: Community photo collection - Statue of Liberty dataset: (a) Subset of the collection of images given to the system - for our co-segmentation algorithm we use a subset of 15 images spanning a large field of view from a collection of 1600 images; (b) Resulting silhouettes after co-segmentation (in cyan color); (c) Some sample novel views of the 3D model (Best viewed in color).

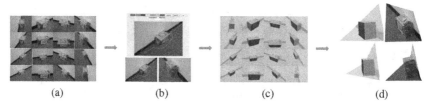

(a)   (b)   (c)   (d)

Fig. 3.10: Scribble based 3D reconstruction: (a) Input images (Image selected by user shown in yellow box); (b) User interactions to indicate the surfaces in the scene; (c) Scene co-segmentation of all images by using the idea of 3D scribbles to propagate scene geometry; (d) Some sample novel views of the reconstruction of the scene, with and without texture (Best viewed in color).

different surfaces in the scene are used to render a planar reconstruction of the scene by performing a surface level co-segmentation of the scene in the group of images.

Background. Automatic 3D reconstruction algorithms [10, 17, 21], have been shown to work well with a large collection of images. When the number of input images is restricted, these automatic algorithms fail to produce a dense/complete reconstruction. There are a number of multiview stereo algorithms which try to obtain a dense depth map for the scene from a set of images [18]. However, multi-view stereo algorithms are known to be slow and with a small set of images the reconstruction is usually incomplete, leaving holes on textureless surfaces and specular reflections. In order to improve the reconstruction, some algorithms make planar approximations to the scene [9, 19]. This allows for more visually pleasing reconstructions. However, these algorithms use features such as strong edges and lines which may be absent in textureless surfaces or non-planar objects (like walls, trees, people, etc). This has led to interactive algorithms. Prior interactive reconstruction algorithms require involved user-interactions ranging from providing feature correspondence to marking edges, plane boundaries and detailed line models of the scene [4, 12, 20].

Algorithm. An overview of our algorithm [14] is illustrated in Fig. 3.10. It allows the user to pick any image and provide scribbles indicating planar surfaces and non-planar objects in the scene, via a modified version of the iCoseg GUI as shown in Fig. 3.11. By extending the binary co-segmentation formulation, we use the scribbles to learn an appearance model for each surface and then, formulate the multi-class segmentation task as an energy minimization problem over superpixels, solved via graph-cuts. This scene segmentation along with the sparse 3D point cloud from structure-from-motion (SFM) helps define the geometry of the scene.

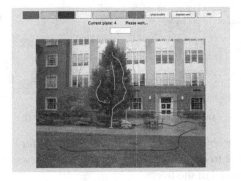

Fig. 3.11: The user interface to provide scribbles to indicate the surfaces and objects in the scene (Best viewed in color).

Rendering non-planar objects via object co-segmentation. The algorithm described so far renders a planar reconstruction of the scene. As stated earlier, non-planar objects in the scene have been identified by the user via scribbles. Recent automatic approaches [11, 15] can also be used for this purpose. We estimate an approximate planar proxy for the object, which helps position the object as part of the rendered scene. We then treat the scribbles corresponding to the non-planar object as foreground scribbles and all other scribbles as background scribbles and use the object-of-interest 3D-modeling algorithm discussed in Section 3.2 to obtain a 3D *visual hull* of the non-planar object. These stages of the algorithm are illustrated in Fig. 3.12. The scene co-segmentation also allows us to create a composite texture map for the scene covering up holes due to occlusions as shown in Fig. 3.13a resulting in the final reconstruction shown in Fig. 3.13b.

Once the algorithm generates the 3D reconstruction, the user can provide more scribbles to indicate new or previously occluded planes, and improve the result, thus closing the loop on our interactive 3D reconstruction algorithm. For more details about the algorithm the reader is referred to Kowdle *et al.* [14].

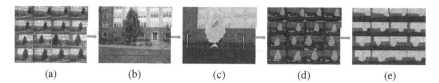

(a)   (b)   (c)   (d)   (e)

Fig. 3.12: Outdoor scene with occlusion: (a) Input images (Image selected by user shown in yellow box); (b) User interactions; (c) Resulting scene segmentation with the additional interactions to indicate surface connectedness (white scribbles shown in black circles) and non-planar objects (magenta scribble shown in blue scribble); (d) Object co-segmentation (foreground non-planar object in yellow); (e) Scene co-segmentation by using 3D scribbles to propagate scene geometry (Best viewed in color).

(a)   (b)

Fig. 3.13: Non-planar objects: (a) Composite texture map for the scene (top) allows covering up holes due to occlusions (ellipse); (b) Novel views of the reconstruction with a volumetric model of the tree.

Results. We demonstrate this application on a number of scenes (both indoor and outdoor) rendering visually pleasing, complete reconstructions. Fig. 3.10d shows the result on a scene with featureless surfaces. Fig. 3.14 how more results on such planar scenes. The algorithm also renders non-planar objects satisfactorily, as we show with the tree in the outdoor scene in Fig. 3.13b and the person in the indoor scene in Fig. 3.14d.

Clearly, co-segmentation enables a wide range of exciting applications. The topic of co-segmentation is receiving increasing attention in literature, but there are many avenues that lie ahead of us that are yet to be explored. The following chapter touches upon some of these potential future directions.

References

1. Y. Chen and G. Medioni. Object modelling by registration of multiple range images. *Image Vision Comput.*, 10(3):145–155, 1992.

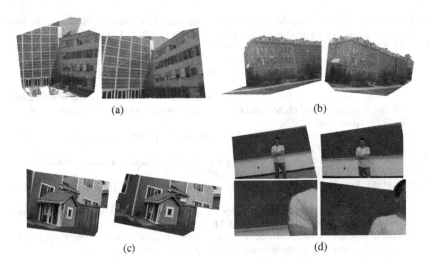

(a)   (b)

(c)   (d)

Fig. 3.14: More results: Novel views of the reconstructed scenes.

2. Z. Chen, H.-L. Chou, and W.-C. Chen. A performance controllable octree construction method. In *ICPR*, pages 1–4, 2008.
3. B. Curless and M. Levoy. A volumetric method for building complex models from range images. In *SIGGRAPH '96: Proceedings of the 23rd annual conference on Computer graphics and interactive techniques*, pages 303–312. ACM, 1996.
4. P. Debevec, C. Taylor, and J. Malik. Modeling and rendering architecture from photographs: A hybrid geometry- and image-based approach. In *SIGGRAPH*, pages 11–20, 1996.
5. Y.-H. Fang, H.-L. Chou, and Z. Chen. 3d shape recovery of complex objects from multiple silhouette images. *Pattern Recogn. Lett.*, 24(9-10):1279–1293, 2003.
6. A. W. Fitzgibbon, G. Cross, and A. Zisserman. Automatic 3d model construction for turntable sequences. In *Proceedings of SMILE Workshop on Structure from Multiple Images in Large Scale Environments*, volume 1506, pages 154–170, 1998.
7. K. Forbes, F. Nicolls, G. de Jager, and A. Voigt. Shape-from-silhouette with two mirrors and an uncalibrated camera. In *ECCV*, pages 165–178, 2006.
8. J.-S. Franco and E. Boyer. Exact polyhedral visual hulls. In *BMVC*, volume 1, pages 329–338, 2003.
9. Y. Furukawa, B. Curless, S. Seitz, and R. Szeliski. Reconstructing building interiors from images. In *ICCV*, 2009.
10. Y. Furukawa and J. Ponce. Accurate, dense, and robust multi-view stereopsis. *PAMI*, 32:1362–1376, 2010.
11. D. Gallup, J. Frahm, and M. Pollefeys. Piecewise planar and non-planar stereo for urban scene reconstruction. In *CVPR*, 2010.
12. A. Hengel, A. R. Dick, T. ThormŁhlen, B. Ward, and P. H. S. Torr. Videotrace: rapid interactive scene modelling from video. *ACM Trans. Graph.*, 26(3):86, 2007.
13. A. Kowdle, D. Batra, W.-C. Chen, and T. Chen. Model: Interactive co-segmentation for object of interest 3d modeling. In *Workshop on Reconstruction and Modeling of Large-Scale 3D Virtual Environments at European Conference on Computer Vision*, 2010.
14. A. Kowdle, Y. Chang, D. Batra, and T. Chen. Scribble based interactive 3d reconstruction via scene cosegmentation. In *ICIP*, 2011.
15. F. Lafarge, R. Keriven, M. Brédif, and V. Hiep. Hybrid multi-view reconstruction by jump-diffusion. In *CVPR*, 2010.
16. M. Levoy, K. Pulli, B. Curless, S. Rusinkiewicz, D. Koller, L. Pereira, M. Ginzton, S. Anderson, J. Davis, J. Ginsberg, J. Shade, and D. Fulk. The digital michelangelo project: 3d scanning of large statues. In *Siggraph*, pages 131–144, 2000.

17. M. Pollefeys, L. Van Gool, M. Vergauwen, F. Verbiest, K. Cornelis, J. Tops, and R. Koch. Visual modeling with a hand-held camera. *IJCV*, V59(3):207–232, 2004.
18. S. M. Seitz, B. Curless, J. Diebel, D. Scharstein, and R. Szeliski. A comparison and evaluation of multi-view stereo reconstruction algorithms. In *CVPR*, volume 1, pages 519–528, 2006.
19. S. Sinha, D. Steedly, and R. Szeliski. Piecewise planar stereo for image-based rendering. In *ICCV*, 2009.
20. S. Sinha, D. Steedly, R. Szeliski, M. Agrawala, and M. Pollefeys. Interactive 3d architectural modeling from unordered photo collections. *ACM Transactions on Graphics (Proceedings of SIGGRAPH Asia 2008)*, 2008.
21. N. Snavely, S. Seitz, and R. Szeliski. Photo tourism: Exploring photo collections in 3d. In *SIGGRAPH*, pages 835–846, 2006.
22. J. Starck and A. Hilton. Surface capture for performance-based animation. *IEEE Computer Graphics and Applications*, 27(3):21–31, 2007.
23. R. Szeliski. Rapid octree construction from image sequences. *CVGIP: Image Understanding*, 58(1):23–32, 1993.
24. D. Vlasic, I. Baran, W. Matusik, and J. Popović. Articulated mesh animation from multi-view silhouettes. In *SIGGRAPH*, pages 1–9. ACM, 2008.
25. L. Zhang, B. Curless, and S. M. Seitz. Rapid shape acquisition using color structured light and multi-pass dynamic programming. *3DPVT*, page 24, 2002.

Chapter 4
Future of Co-segmentation

Abstract Co-segmentation is a new topic which has only been recently introduced into the computer vision community. In Chapter 2 we have discussed the interactive co-segmentation algorithm in detail and in Chapter 3 we covered some of the interesting applications of co-segmentation but there is more to explore in this field. In this chapter, we discuss the future of co-segmentation, the algorithm and its application.

Appearance models. One of the key insights we have gained through the prior work in co-segmentation is that appearance models play a critical role in the algorithm. The ability to describe the object of interest via a discriminative appearance model that is robust to changes in lighting, illumination, view-point and occlusion is critical for co-segmentation to work in real unconstrained image collections. However, most prior works have relied on relatively weak appearance models based on color distributions in the images. We are yet to explore richer features like shape or contour descriptors. For example, the task of human or people co-segmentation is much more challenging than generic object co-segmentation. The variability in clothing causes appearance models based on colour/texture to become essentially meaningless. In this scenario, body contours/shape becomes a very powerful cue.

While co-segmentation has so far been explored for a group of unstructured yet topically related images, we believe the core algorithm can be applied to other modalities as well. In particular, a practical application of co-segmentation is in medical imaging. Radiologists look at CT scans to identify tumors and with the improved quality of these scans identifying the tumors is becoming easier. A useful representation for surgeons is to have is a 3D model which shows the structure of the tumor. We believe co-segmentation can help in such a scenario. By indicating the location of the tumor (perhaps interactively) to the algorithm, we can learn a model for the tumor and co-segment the tumor in each slice of the CT scan. These segmentations can now allow for a volumetric 3D representation of the tumor. The key to applying co-segmentation to applications such as this is to define a discriminative representation for the foreground in this modality.

Thus exploring representative and discriminative appearance models based on the modality and application will be critical to the success of co-segmentation.

Beyond the binary formulation. The task of co-segmentation has been well explored for the binary formulation of foreground vs. background. However, as we presented in Chapter 3, it can be extended to multi-label problems. This multi-label formulation can help existing vision problems. One example is simultaneous localization and mapping (SLAM) which is an active area of research in robotics. A well-known problem in SLAM methods is that the features (or landmarks) used can sometimes drift or become lost as the robots move through the environment, since matching and tracking these features is hard. Using the multi-label co-segmentation formulation one can track multiple objects in the environment, treating the whole object as landmarks thus providing much more support. The key issue to address here is speed. These applications demand near real-time processing of the visual data and thus fast, efficient approximate algorithms are needed for co-segmentation.

Co-recognition and semantic co-segmentation. Object recognition is one of the fundamental problems in computer vision. One sub-problem that been receiving increasing attention in recent works is that of multi-view recognition, *i.e.* leveraging multiple images that capture the object from different view-points to learn a "view-point aware" representation for the object. We believe this is a scenario where co-segmentation can help. Access to an accurate spatial support corresponding to the same object in multiple images allows for the extraction of discriminative shape and appearance features. Moreover, recognition and the incorporation of semantic knowledge can also in turn help co-segmentation. For instance, in order to co-segment cars, incorporating semantic information such as context (is there a street in the image? and horizon? buildings?) and geometric support (what is the car resting on?) have proved to be very useful.

Pushing the limits of unsupervised techniques. In the active learning formulation in Chapter 2.2, we showed that given the user input on one image, we can reliably recommend the most informative regions for the user to provide inputs thereby reducing the user effort. The future of co-segmentation is in stretching the limits of unsupervised object co-segmentation algorithms to further reduce the user effort. While the notion of an object of interest is ill-posed without a user in the loop, recent works in unsupervised co-segmentation have shown that if the background changes in appearance more drastically than the foreground then one can automatically segment out the foreground object.

The open issue to address is how an unsupervised algorithm might handle a scenario where the background does not change drastically, or a scenario where appearance models between the foreground and background overlap heavily. It is in this regime that better appearance models, using higher-level reasoning such as context and semantics, and intelligently incorporating the user in the loop would all fit in. This is where we believe the field of co-segmentation is headed.